# Untouched Landscape

poems

Hideko Sueoka

Clare Songbirds Publishing House Poetry Series
ISBN 978-1-947653-27-6
Clare Songbirds Publishing House
*Untouched Landscape*© 2018 Hideko Sueoka
All Rights Reserved. Clare Songbirds Publishing House retains right to reprint.
Permission to reprint individual poems must be obtained from the author who owns the copyright.

Printed in the United States of America
FIRST EDITION

140 Cottage Street
Auburn, New York 13021
www.ClareSongbirdspub.com

cover photos by TAXI agency ©*2018*

# Contents

| | |
|---|---|
| Cherry Blossoms | 7 |
| Quakes | 8 |
| Spring Bird | 9 |
| Owl | 10 |
| Ruddy Kingfisher | 12 |
| Breakthrough with English | 13 |
| Lost Persona | 14 |
| In Entr'acte between Dusk and Dawn | 15 |
| Trails of White Hare | 16 |
| The Lilac | 18 |
| Amber and Old Letter | 19 |
| Different Hopes | 20 |
| Ice Cube | 21 |
| The Remains of Breath | 22 |
| Around Fire | 23 |
| Awakening in Funeral | 24 |
| Aubade in Finland | 25 |
| Flat Peach | 26 |
| Birch Sap | 27 |
| Orange Episodes | 28 |
| Lighthouse Keeper | 29 |
| Cat's Cradle | 30 |
| Doer of Fasting | 31 |
| Kaleidoscope | 32 |
| Where is My Home? | |
|    I. Robert Frank: Trolley – New Orleans 1955 | 33 |
|    II. Bruce Davidson: South Wales 1965 | 34 |
|    III. Lisette Model: Blind Man with Guitar | 35 |
| Before Breaking Stillness | 36 |
| Moon | 38 |
| Weather Man | 39 |

The author gracefully acknowledges to the editors and publishers of the following magazines and anthologies, online or/and printed, where the poems first appeared, some of which were later changed slightly for this chapbook.

"Owl" – *Coffee-House Poetry* and anthology of the *Forward Book of Poetry* 2014 (Faber & Faber)

"Where is My Home?" – *Poetry Kanto* in 2014

"Aubade in Finland" – *Visual Verse* in 2015

"Ruddy King Fisher" – *Ink, Sweat & Tears* in 2015

"Cherry Blossoms" – *Ink, Sweat & Tears* in 2016

*For my family, and for all the people who have supported my poetry writing*

## Cherry Blossoms

My facial colour is dark blue, though in spring.
Oh my, can you see ashy-indigo confetti?

A cherry addict admires pale pink
fluttering down in lambent sunlight.

But through the flyaway organza of misty breath,
my skin hides another complexion

that lurks on the counterfeit surface
in spring frolics. After catharsis of my mind,

unknown beauty you can find in me
bright blue – like cranesbill, grape hyacinth, catmint.

## Quakes

Raft on roof, and roof on raft, and upside down.
Quake and tsunami whirl, spin my landscape.
Life turns to death in this chaotic town.

Swallowed up, the humble and renown.
The raft cannot be Noah's ark, atop the cape.
Raft on roof, and roof on raft, and upside down.

Red and yellow signboards lie face down.
A cradle bobs and takes a coffin's shape.
Life turns to death in this chaotic town.

Oars turn to driftwood, souls flow on to drown.
They have no destination, nor escape.
Raft on roof, and roof on raft, and upside down.

The colour of the world is muddy brown.
Like underground, the world has lost all shape.
Life turns to death in this chaotic town.

Come back, you dead, wherever you have flown.
Words fail and stunned, we can but stand and gape.
Raft on roof, and roof on raft, and upside down.
Life turns to death in this chaotic town.

## Spring Bird, White-eye

Buds bloom in this moratorium of winter cold
and wings open. Near shrubbery along an alley,
flimsy plum blossom petals drip softly
onto my nape. Overhead an olive bird
with white-trimmed eyes pecks at lemon pollen,
arching its plumpness into a sickle,
clinging to a wispy twig upside-down
like a trapezist hanging from the trapeze.
The white-eye is just a limber ornament in the still tree.
Oblivious to Lent, how you crave a sip of nectar!

Your partner scatters Elysian notes as it wanders
through the crisp day, seeking an uncertain realm,
the notes echoing through a roof garden, to a pagoda.
Spring stirs in the couple's quest for beauty.

# Owl
*For Mr. G. P. and Mr. G. A.*

**I.**
Now I work without that sign following
D, prior to F. I follow you,
writing about an owl fascinating
my soul, Mr. G. P., far from haiku.
Did you catch calls of an owl in a park
in Paris sounding again and again?
You did? I, too, pick up this song at dark
singing not-'twhoo' but 'coo hmm' in misty rain.
Did you think of this owl as a symbol
of sharp-sighted wisdom in Paris?
In Shanghai this owl signals sin and ill
and bad luck, on a par with cannabis.
In your world, if an Asian owl should light
on you, would you call it or avoid it?

**II.**
Mr. G. A., your brilliant translation
A VOID migrating, landing on my hand.
I, too, look for 'hoot' in variation,
using lipography just as you did.
With your notation, 'twhoo pht' 'twhoo pfft'
   'twhoo pht'   'twhoo pfft' 'twhooo'.
Do you hark to hoots of an Asian owl?
With my notation, 'coo hmm' 'coo hmmm' 'coo hmm'
   'coo hmmm' 'cooo'.
Do you grasp such whoops as fair or foul?
An individual ululation
   has multi-marks and plural compound chords
varying on points, skirting all canons
that control thoughts, though producing discords.
'Hmm', 'twhoo pht' 'coo pht' 'twhooo pht' 'cooo pht'
   'twhoo hmm' 'coo hmm' 'twhoo pfft' 'coo pfft'.
How would you hoot owl's fuzzy sound? Just how?

## III.
Thoughtful old owl, you stand in a brown oak.
You do not talk, you do but mull and gird;
You do but mull and gird, you do not talk;
Not all can do as you do, thoughtful bird.
O awful owl, you scowl in a ginkgo.
You go off, swooping out, and up and down.
And a dark bass doom thrums in your lingo.
How swift is your flight, how grim is your frown!
In soft wind, twhoo by twhoo, 'twhoo pht' 'twhoo pht'
  'twhoo pfft' 'twhoo'
is 'coo hmm' 'coo hmm' 'coo hmmm' 'coo hmmm'
  'cooo hm' 'cooo hm' 'coo' 'coo' 'hoot',
or 'uu ho' 'uuu ho' 'uuuu ho' 'uu ho' 'uuu'.
And your singular cry grows variant.
And although mystical your haunting call,
owl is owl is owl for you — that is all.

\*Mr. G. P. is Georges Perec who wrote the novel
'La Disparition' ('A VOID').
Mr. G. A. is Gilbert Adair who translated the novel into English.

## Ruddy Kingfisher

You follow the edge of the bird's stringy trills pace by pace;
the sound descending into rank bracken ferns
and datura flowers under leaves of wild papayas.

The tremolos of calls reroll and re-echo
in your ears through humid monsoon bringing rain
as if in *Bellinati*'s music in deep woodlands

at dawn and dusk as in moments when Eos and Nyx
wander West to East, try to explore
untrampled places. The goddesses search for their calls.

You can't yet catch the finicky bird burning, sliding
in mid-air, not a phoenix but a real omnivore
ingesting a striped ant on the ground, a toad

in a jade stream, something of what is scrummy, eerie.
You hear that its petite tail flirts with itself
on a splotchy perch, percussing emptiness.

In the ancient manuscript, you once came across
an image of its red beak like a sheath,
without hearing your vibrations of its mystic notes.

With aridness in March, bowed moss loses
a slight sheen, sapless leaves quiver lightly
on branches, each frond is barren for a moment.

On such a day, the wings guide fickle squall
to sleeping jungles with trills. It's old lore,
today the thirsty woods await dear water

from the sky. Its flapping shadow isn't yet known to you.
Cold dew drops on your forehead. Fresh showers
   come, fall and fall:
transparent song brings prayers, then rain, then green.

*Bellinati*—Paulo Bellinati (born in 1950) is a Brazilian classical guitarist.

## Breakthrough with English

A cell is my tiny office. Every day,
every night, even on Sunday, I've been immured
in this cell filled with only cold words like stones, shingle,
pebbles, cooled lava, scabrous rocks with tints
   and patterns.
They have no body temperature, no hearts,
no emotions, like carcasses, like dead men and women
in a chapel of rest, a mortuary, a graveyard.
How many volumes have I translated for
   my routine work:
patents – marmoreal blocks? By climbing up
a ladder made of words, I may reach Venus, Aries.
Nevertheless, once reading Yeats and Keats,
there was something like a breakthrough in me –
collapse of dead, cold words in myself. My soul
might indwell in the pages where warm blood circulates
in poems in English: non-mother tongue. All words
with temperature should emerge as natural,
alive and moving, moving towards a sigh, a smile,
and tears. The cell starts to breathe under the spring sun,
turning to a forest of leafy birches with flycatchers.

## Lost Persona
*For Hannah Arendt*

My people are a flock of sluggish sheep
that crops pasture plants en masse near a cedar
and turns their faces to *yes* though hoping a leap
when changing the direction under the head's order.

My people are a herd of still zebras
that looks about red oat grass on the scrubland,
and nods, *yes*, in unison, in dread of cheetahs,
to trite thoughts of the leader, with nothing planned.

It's hard to find *I*, self, and ego here.
Bereft. The skill of conformity is preferred.
And likeness is right, unlikeness the worst.
And before me, think always of the taste of others.

If taking back a persona in situ,
can the stout self bring untold words to light to you?

## In Entr'acte between Dusk and Dawn

In the reign of night, you sparkle
from tip to tip of upswept teal blades

near the marsh. You change to a firefly:
awake, come from a reservoir.

An airy chart is unfolded
for mating, for love, for bliss.

With elytra, soaring beyond
Logos – you had as a human

but you don't have it. Low glow, no glow
inducing hypnosis or cloudland.

Fluorescent blurs everywhere
in insects' nocturne from nowhere.

They're shiny loci in the dark
on a rain-spattered window.

After a sojourn on dew, your glimmer
becomes a will-o'-the-wisp leaping

to your next incarnation or
new spirit on pellucid water.

# Trails of White Hare

One winter night I wandered through snow
near a hot-springs hotel in a birch woods

where smoke and steam like fleece floated
as faint as black-ink wash on the sheet.

Flurries no longer swirled; the appearance
showed bluish silver. Stillness awaited wind

and sound sinking into pure white. Frozen air
put my senses to snooze. Blurred hours.

Pale rays seeped through extant leaves, endlessly-spread.
So deep in my ears, the sleeping woods.

I gingerly searched for something near and far:
Not an owl, not a fox. It split the air;

fleet-footed, left to right, white on white, too fast to catch.
A presence was left, moving like a mere breath.

A whirring of wind. A thing wafting up,
soft and smooth as cotton. Then gone somewhere.

And strolling about the barn, I bumped against
a broken signboard. 'Caution, bears!' in the gloom.

Shivers seized me. To a close thick trunk
I scurried, then mounted a rugged rock.

A thing came quickly. It didn't take shape.
It hurried off and soon hid.

Hush. Rustling, lisping. Branches were leafless here.
Well, manifestly, it was an animal.

Staring at the steep path, there were tracks
of a white hare. I traced them to the top,

chasing a sequence of tiny steps, a big leap,
and back. Then step by step the tracks faded.

All at once there were none. Nothing
on the gentle slope, but snow, sickly light.

The full moon seemed a circular mirror
reflecting my uncertain feelings.

I felt that the dark shadows were the hare,
tried to catch it, but couldn't. Gloom was a crescent.

Fog flowed away and no traces of trails
remained. All melted in snow and moon.

## The Lilac

In threads of purple hue, petals of the lilac
softly whisper her puzzle but no one listens any longer,
even if swaying a bunch of blossoms.
Faint voices through her pipes don't reach each ear;
even if they're caught, passers-by might feel frivolous.

Shades of the lilac are a sort of dusk sky,
a sort of ripe flare of life. Her ambivalence can't
be said with colour, scent. But the shrub wants to speak
before a fickle puff carries her murmuring,
before the mauve glories wither away.

## Amber and Old Letter

Amongst forgotten bric-a-brac, an umber spider
remains still, a fossil in the firm resin of pine trees.
Little eternity trapped in a hyaline holder
that had hardened at a slow pace through layered times
in a dull nugget on a forlorn seashore.
Beneath the arthropod, the sallow postcard from Grandma
sleeps. The small maw is coiled by ochre thrums
of cloud like a broken web, shining with marmalade jam-
tinted streaks. Without man's hand, the stuffed insect.

Upon opening the paulownia drawer by chance,
each recall of the relics shimmers, arises with faint sight
   and ripens with night. The past waylays me from the
   remote mist. The fixed thorax and neat script
   of the dead in darkness:
mementos await to be found once more in silence
   and light.

## Different Hopes
## — Night and Day —

Which gives me a feeling of comfort, night or day?
Unable to answer. Hard to say and fix. Both I love.
Nightqueen flower and Mayflower. Both bear fruit.
If choosing one, it would kill one beautiful creation.
    Deadly acute.

Which eyes catch me with a feeling of fear,
closed or opened?
Absolutely doubtful. Neither puts me at ease.
Nightmare or daydream. Neither leads me
to calming stories.
Whichever state I'm in, the opposite brings the escape.

## Ice Cube

A cool die without pips is protean
in a tumbler on a worn-out coaster.

At first, flawless vertices and sharp edges
in Gin, Maker's Mark, Balblair with a short

damped ting-a-ling. The pips become blebs
and all gone in the limpid fluid that dilutes.

For your love for distilled drink, I make here
ice cubes that wait for a subtle fragrance,

each one is too slick to easily fix
like an avalanche in an alpine terrain.

Open the fridge-freezer and pour *evian*
in a tray with cavities to slowly grow it

toward a set of chilled quartz cells in rows,
toward frozen boxes with effulgence.

Hard rime like frosted conifer foliage
emerges step by step with the thorough bass

of a fridge motor. From liquid to solid:
be still as a statue, death of warmth.

Posthumously, the rigid world appears
to be crystalline resin below zero.

You put the finished cubes into the glass, then,
squint closely at Glenfiddich on the rocks

before drinking. Leisurely melting.
Amber streaks run on, gently twist and sink.

Ice is back to liquid. You taste the flux,
imagining you're water flowing to somewhere.

## The Remains of Breath

It's connection time between night and day—
an icy December dawn. First blackness gone.

Out of dim dreams, out of warmth in soft quilts
we get up and try to portray the brisk world.

While half asleep or half awake intermittently
in utter stillness without the neighbour's greyhound barking,

thin steam from our lips soon vanishes
in the winter yard dappled with hoar frost.

To opaque shapes of firs before us, keen air passes.
Inhale slowly, widening the stiff midriff.

Charge latent energy in our bodies where capillaries
are fresh, followed by a short pause.

The wind leads out breathing to oaks, to lichens.
Exhale, not-puffing, shrinking the belly with concentration,

without tension, then it is iambic
heart pulse far from crow screams in triple beat.

Our breath paths aren't squiggly but nearly straight,
unravelled, coruscant, and melted in sun's bright rays.

## Around Fire

A flare sways and shimmers in stillness.
I strike a match to make a fire
casting back to lost clips and outtakes.

In front of the copse of lush beeches,
in the flicker of a flame of burnt
tinder – drab bark and ochre straw,

O, grandma, gran is there. She wafts
in silk tulle stained tangerine, gone.
Snatched by a salamander. To where?

A flare sways and shimmers in stillness.
I ignite driftwood that was alone
adrift from tide to tide, to the coast.

A bit far from the landlocked bay,
pieces of the wood are a torch
lighting loneliness with ripples' thrum.

A glimmer of a fishing boat
pops up, a phantasmagoria
of dolphins and hawksbills flickers.

A flare sways and shimmers in stillness.
Beside an inglenook, I crouch,
reread old letters with crackling sounds.

Ah well, I croon, ah well, stare at
ghostly shades of flames, then follow
longhand, forgotten names, attached stamps.

I put past sadness on paper
in fire that will be embers and ashes.

## Awakening in Funeral
*For Charles Simic*

Creamy Labrador Retriever with a short horn.
Creamy Labrador Retriever with curled hackles.
Creamy Labrador Retriever on florid clouds.
Creamy Labrador Retriever on teal-blue water.
These aren't in Max Ernst's maze.
Night views below lamps.
Emersion of tears and trite materials.

Inside a parlour for funeral with three
Venetian windows where a mourner hangs her head
and draws tap-top drapes, the ceremony is held
when sight fails through the hue of squid ink.
On a pane, one bead is combined with another,
projecting reflections of bizarre figures.
Mourners who dress in black can't look at
each other straight with sore hearts, biting their lips.

The blind people depart out from there
with guide dogs wagging their tails without barking,
then scattering into wide fields with no shadows
of what danced and stopped openly in daytime.
The dead man who was visually impaired
has shut eyes forever; will tour unmapped places.
The darkness makes the sense of ear acute.
The lightlessness wakens hidden scenes.

I knock, unlock the postern for my return,
go out, and crouch down in a murky parking lot;
Inky mongrel pug popping up from shrubs.
Haematite-crystal Bombay(*) on a pavement.
Raven with glossy oil-scarfed wings.
The beasts! The melanin beasts zoom to a halogen light.

*Bombay– Bombay cat

## Aubade in Finland

At Oulu, mysterious days of a solstitial camp
so full of awe and fuss with the midnight sun
that dyes a white sink in hues,
brings a soon-gone night to run through a window.
At dawn the goblin Lempo hides in damp

himself for lost short darkness with auroral cool dew.
In bungalows, he betrays people and plays a trick
with a bath mirror in slant light as his eyes, his view
that reflects from capricious expressions, the quick
of the campers who are riveted by the reflection.
They squeeze toothpaste, brush their teeth as if staring at
unseen Lempo who watches their frenzied to-dos that
are traced like sleepwalkers in a daydream, recollection.
And dawn again. With his off-the-cuff wiles to
get amnesia, their retreat is over. Here lies a
collage of tap running, things left behind in ice blue.

# Flat Peach

Not seen in Tokyo, but sold at stalls
   in Hong Kong and London.
A lot of the fruits on a worn pine table - flower bouquet.

In a shambles of claps, loud calls, noises echoing
beneath the low roof, among sausages, greens, mackerels,

I picked up, bought two ripe flat peaches piled up
in a crate with fresh skin mixedly dyed pale yolk and pink

like the cheek of a newborn baby on a bassinet,
imagining the charming blossoms of the fruit

shook in spring wind in an orchard, the crushed nectar
with luscious aroma on my tongue on a sultry day.

In my hotel room, I placed, stared at these dainties
in front of a trifold mirror that reflected Chinese

interiors, carpet, antique desk, hanging scroll. I bit
a big one. Yes, I ate plenty of rich folk tales

of this ambrosia. The taste was familiar, similar
to the Japanese one, soon induced a doze in a chair.

After taking a nap, I could not know whether I was in
a dream. Via the window, dusk light seeped into the room.

Everything was fused in colour shades of lotus flower,
so full of sweet scent. The evening world was all
   the peach.

## Birch Sap

Birch, you sanctified me. I blessed, savoured
your gift, uncoloured liquid with delicate taste.
My delightful moment- as if drinking wine
with a chalice and an elixir of life.
Sap tapping is mastering patience. A drip dropped
on drips - the juice healed me as a tisane.
Now I traipse over the snow land around you
by drawing in my mind with pointillism
reminiscence of hues of serrated leaves
in summer, autumn – lime-green to blonde,
and gold to mint, then moss-green to rose-red
with echoic crying of black-backed wagtails.
I see there your dryad has lamented
your dead mates - tall poplars, bird cherries, oaks,
your dryad has wept over their lost voices.
Snow hides bygones and your whippy branch
that cocks the ear to wind whir, rillet sound.
My thirst waits for the spring harvest. Imagine
a mug brimming with your water – grace.

## Orange Episodes

Gilded Venus - a lustrous orange reminds me
of neroli oil and Cointreau in a cocktail,
beautiful enough to dizzy my vision.
Well, slice it, pick it. The stare inspires gyring dreams.

One short cut. A fob watch inside the tweed waistcoat,
antique yet working after your grandad's death.
If tick-tock stops, forever silent, your memory to him
might disappear like ashes in the Great Fire of London.

One short cut. A circular compass on the warm palm,
essential in a zig-zag trek to a thick maquis
by a tor in Greece where the magnetic field is zero
(I've heard so), the hands whirl and roll.
   No ways to decamp.

One short cut. The rotation of a water wheel
at full-moon night in Amsterdam. Shades of the loci
of the wheel motions spread on the water of the canal.
Hums of the wheel bring a peaceful sleep to creatures.

One short cut. A Ferris wheel in a traveling fun fair
in Malaga, at night, sundry neons of green,
indigo, yellow, and plum bloom, recalling Picasso.
In midnight hours, abstract contours with bridged
  last glows.

## Lighthouse Keeper

A fragment of the Fresnel lens placed on the shelf,
shaped like a chipped crystal ball - he retrieved
on the premises of the beacon, firefly's flare.

An isolated lighthouse itself sleeping in the recall
survives at hand at a ragged path on a headland.
Its tumble-down tower is home in his homecoming

that might be the last visit. Scanning the dead tract,
his eyes narrow against the sun, to a weed grown way.
One gait is a closer gait to bygone solitude.

Unlocking a door padlock, filled with tools –
rusted-out gauges, split fog bells, Jupiter sextant
enfolded with dust and grit. Time's here. It lies still

or it moves. He jerks the eyes to a clouded round
window mirroring the nightmare storm on keeping
his vigil. Tragedy. It cropped up on raging waves.

A prow came out, by and by gone in spindrift.
A fisherman flowed away, a trawler turned turtle.
Wide tides irrupted, swallowed his body and three

that were drowned, turfed out, sunk in dark water again.
Unreturned. The keeper sees the ghost helming
a dory to a turbid shore, then under the under.

Fierce wind, evil night, and death - the daytime limpid sky
forgets all. He goes outside to allay himself.
There's only silence and total disarray.

Broken pieces of lens glass forlorn near the tower.
He flips them away to the choppy sea to put his hours
with the lens to sleep in water for eternity.

## Cat's Cradle

Once she fidgeted with him, twirled him –
theurgy, he could awake, turn into coral,

turtle, melon rind, or stars between
Perseus and Pegasus. He, the loop, murmured,

'Well, Sue, you have no face, no trunk, dead
in a pocket or coffret as tousled wool.'

She played with him alone, opting
to choose Jacob's ladder on a snug rug.

At first, strain him with thumb and pinkie
of each hand. This was the initial style.

Next digits' romp was to shape opening A
that has two triangles and one rhomboid

from above as well as with index fingers
that deftly moved as if striking notes.

Her thumbs sinuously went over and under,
under and over, like skipping a rope.

En route, cat's whiskers inside her tightened,
she imagined a calico cat tiptoeing

in an ill-lit vault, soon vanished, but cat's hairs left.
The pick-up, drop process was tricky bit by bit.

Through some work and break of polygon,
at last, she finished the celestial steps.

Neat crochet. But soon gone like a wisp of steam,
like a breath of God. Back to the loop of string.

## Doer of Fasting

Towards the deep of a mountain full of verdure,
I climbed, stopped at a ragged track, moved ahead
again. To slough off flab and spiritual dust,
towards the retreat, leaving regular chores.

The practice place for my ascetic life
was a one-story dojo in the forest
scilicet apart from worldly affairs,
but was neither a church nor a shrine.

One bowl of sloppy porridge every day.
Austere fare. Alas, this meal was ambrosia
for me. Shortly somewhat sullen, but less than
somewhat wrung-out. Forgotten senses were back.

While bearing up under a pang of hunger
I had to walk between trees not to lose muscle,
this wasn't meditation, far from rumination.
Ordeal. I wasn't a flawless hermit yet.

In a short catnap, a cooing voice came:
'And lo, here, cherry pie, baked potato,
beef stroganoff, chicken tikka masala'.
This whisper recurred in me in the gloomy nook.

My night dream didn't bloom in unripe sleep,
the calmness was calmer in darkness.
I prayed for the early coming of dawn.
But night lingered on so long. I lay awake.

At last I finished the arduous practice,
my body was light, and I preened myself.
My psyche was purified. There, more beautiful
birdsong I'd never heard, in the same green and air.

## Kaleidoscope

Carnation, chandelier, no matter -
What a glorious bloom through mirrors!

In the summer fair, his mother purchased
for him this tin tube exhibiting kilims

with shifting motifs. With his right eye,
he had looked hard at the inside of tunnel

reflecting, rotating patterns with many
small grilles aligned in order through one window.

He turned the body of the toy, imagining
the aurora borealis he'd watched on TV.

No big-bang, no roars. Firework displays
began in front of him in dead silence.

Small bursts of light. There was an arrangement
of painted dandelion pappi

like waiting for the best timing for flight
with a waft of wind towards a utopia.

Small bursts of light. The bottom of the hole
was a stage of spinning umbrellas

with one-hundred-carat diamonds,
with iridescent raindrops spattering down.

Unable to touch quicksilver motions
of visions: shooting stars gone and born and gone.

## Where is My Home?

### I. Robert Frank: Trolley – New Orleans 1955
*(Born in Switzerland)*

To a space where their eyes are out-of-focus,
diffuse as their whispers in raucous air

or as a stellar cloud including a far-off star
and a hollow locale that would be a new one,

the other side of their lives on a trolley
transferring from area to area, the outside

of windows opened to fleeting scenes or
comforting tones of trombone and closed to

shut-out unclear tableaux, allow us to zoom into
their faces showing doze or ennui in one shot,

mysterious, every so often
unfixed emotions can be fixed at a certain

monochrome moment. The overlapped
glass above them rolls mostly on bumpy roads

as if the surface of a puddle rippled
casting back snippy and motley cityscapes

educed in their limbos; splintery flashbacks
are churned with blurred after-images.

Each gaze to a distant point, a puzzle
where light is focused in their shadowlands.

## II. Bruce Davidson: South Wales 1965
*(Born in the United States of America)*

A sphere before evening from the region
where nobody strolls, the dour boy will go to,
encompassed by plume, soot, and adverse dust
spelt with coal, heat, and carbon dioxide.

He, wearing glasses, carries his teddy bear
and baby doll as dead bodies to be
ensconced into a concealed store, they were
quite tame denizens of his colony

away from where weary colliers dig the earth.
The captured view is within a stone's throw
from us; easy to see coke dump, oak death,
and asthma due to coal-dirty air with flow

of noise. The sphere, a sort of Arcadia
he's dreamt of and sought on his own at Rhondda.

\*\*\* *Rhondda — Previous coal mining place in Wales*

### III. Lisette Model: Blind Man with Guitar
*(Born in Austria)*


At the edge of the earth, at lilac dusk
the blind man I know by hearsay has
espied light at a part of the arabesque.

As he plucks strings, he is engrossed in tunes
even if there're rowdies around him;
then making them serene, besotted with his

refrains, melancholic and exotic, slim
child-stumbling paced phrases, every music
he plays he can be taken as a hymn.

His ears are open to voices in any stich
alive to a wind calling, grown silence
pococurante to the public.

His eyes are closed to secular affairs, balance,
clairvoyant to an infant's senses and heart
competent to read the moonlight presence.

Among nocturnal murmurs, his skilled art
blooming in nifty riffs as *When Day is Done*
of Django Reinhardt in Paris, his fingers' dart

lush-flinging winsome dissonances, one
suspended-chord to another, a spate
of passion, an abrupt break, then a pun,

and fret. Tones soon gone with him over the gate.


\*\*\* *Django Reinhardt (1910 – 1953) — Belgian-born French musician of Romani heritage, famous for using only the index and middle fingers of his left hand and establishing his own jazz guitar technique.*

# Before Breaking Stillness
*For Fan Ho*
*nobody detains the sun* – Juan Gelman

One moment of stillness –
the border between night and day.
The navy sky breaks, the near-horizon splits with
   clear hues.
No policemen, no citizens walk in this city now.
Even no glum faces of passers-by sweating in mid-June.

Metallic rails for trams gleam on the wet street,
like parallel traces of figure skaters on ice.
Dew with cool air rinses yesterday's everything
and the sunrise light illuminates ways of people in
   Hong Kong.

A pulled rickshaw travels slowly. No passengers therein:
empty seat. The driver runs with wheels, passes over
the rails while moving his lips. His low soliloquy flows
in wind, sunk under the steep pavement full of memories.

The handle for pulling the vehicle is decrepit,
he stoops by hard work under signboards filling
   the mid-air.
How many wheels has he exchanged for his rickshaw?
How many angry persons, joyful persons has he carried?

Shutters of banks, stores are closed yet like eyelids
of a sleeping woman. After scavengers collect litter,
a vehicle goes ahead fast in front of the old buildings,
only advertising paper and dusts swirl therebetween.

In this sunrise-flooded city, birdsong comes
   from somewhere.
Doves fly, chase love. Again, sighs, tears,
   and smiles are born.
The street is gradually filled with noise, voices, screeches
with mellow smell of food, spices with shadow of
   human beings.

## Moon
*For Susan Derges*

Now Susan's focus is a lensless scene
whose reconjured world is hers in slanting moonlight
that draws water rings on water
with imperfect plumpness.
Leaving a flash in her studio, shunning the sun,
catching the pale phase with the serene lunar mare.
A puff of winds is ephemeral breathing
that produces the interference of little ripples
with a colour change from silver to caesious.
Weeds fuse to blocky clouds in an aqua mirror
whereon borders are fuzzy, misty. Still but modified.
The shadow might loom out beyond the fluid.
The moon gift is a cyano-hallucination.
Grey shrouds make the state of matter vague,
not *yes*-or-*no*, but between *yes* and *no*.

## Weather Man
*For Evgenia Arbugaeva*

His space is in Russian hues, Arctic stillness,
his space is like a chilly dungeon
where bright light does not sluice his solitude
at the fallow outpost at a low altitude.
He notes down snowfall, temperatures, maelstroms.
In front of a transceiver, his voice echoes with a frown.
Nor forth, nor back, the alabaster view of an icy field
enriches feeble sunshine; olive rays, teal blue rays shield
the decayed remnants of white nights and the rays move
so that they are not as they were. Soft skins,
   gusts removed.
With iron crampons, he gathers polar data
outside, walks towards the frozen river delta,
then looks up at alary clouds on snow-covered scree.
He says, 'oh, tiny epiphany, aurora, see'.

**Hideko Sueoka** is Japanese, living in Tokyo, writing poems in English while working as a technical and legal translator for a long time. She has learnt English poetry with English poetry teachers, translators living in Japan, attended ARVON workshops and others in the UK and Portugal, and Fishtrap workshop in the US, and completed poetry writing courses in Writers' Centre Norwich in the UK. She was the winner of the 2013 Troubadour International Poetry Competition, and her winning poem *Owl* was highly commended in the Forward Prize 2014. Her translation on photography *Shigeichi Nagano-Magazine Work 60s* was published in 2009 (Heibonsha, Japan), and her poems have been published in magazines, mainly in the UK.

www.ingramcontent.com/pod-product-compliance
Lightning Source LLC
Chambersburg PA
CBHW012007120526
44592CB00040B/2660